Marianne Reyes

Organisational learning and development during a recession

How eBay, Apple and Google foster organisational learning and development

Marianne Reyes

Organisational learning and development during a recession

How eBay, Apple and Google foster organisational learning and development

GRIN Verlag

Bibliografische Information der Deutschen Nationalbibliothek: Die Deutsche Bibliothek
verzeichnet diese Publikation in der Deutschen Nationalbibliografie; detaillierte bibliografische Daten sind im Internet über http://dnb.d-nb.de/ abrufbar.

1. Auflage 2010
Copyright © 2010 GRIN Verlag
http://www.grin.com/
Druck und Bindung: Books on Demand GmbH, Norderstedt Germany
ISBN 978-3-640-85161-4

This paper critically evaluates whether learning and development is an unnecessary expense during a credit crunch. The first part of the paper gives a brief definition and overview in terms of training and development. Furthermore, when it comes to development it is worth bearing in mind that it is a far reaching concept with many different aspects which does not only include training. That is where organisational learning and culture come into the play. In order to promote understanding, the paper refers to practical examples of some of the most successful organisations such as eBay, Apple and Google.

In order to promote understanding it is crucial to make a clear distinction between training and development, because both words have a different meaning. According to Martin and Jackson (2002, p. 145), training can be described as *a process through which individuals are helped to learn a skill or technique.* Development, on the other hand, *occurs as a result of learning and can happen in any number of ways: for example: through training events or via the methods of coaching, mentoring, planned and unplanned experience in the workplace and so forth* (Sadler-Smith, 2006, p. 10).

The question which arises is why training and development is so important? Without doubt, due to the constant introduction of sophisticated technology, the world is changing faster than ever. Hence, it is of the utmost importance to provide training opportunities for staff at all levels in the organisational hierarchy in order to enhance the knowledge of both individuals and the organisation as a whole. But this can be quite challenging in times of a financial crisis, because many organisations try their best to cut down costs. In fact, the rigorous solution companies are likely to come up with is to scrap training and development for their employees.

Martin Clarke, director of General Management Programmes in Cranfield School of Management, stresses that *it is vital to give your top people the support they need, especially during economic downturns* (Clarke, 2009) because a *well-trained and skilled workforce will be instrumental in supporting organisations during the downturn as well as after economic recovery and growth resumes.* (Ambition, 2010)

A survey which was conducted by Boston Consulting Group and the European Association of People Management found out that cutting costs with regard to training and development in a recession can have a serious impact on the organisation from a long-term perspective (Strack et al, 2009).

In the first glance training and development might be regarded as a luxury investment in times of a recession. However, if organisations seek to be successful they need to realise that there are much more aspects than training and development in order to cope with external threats. A critical determinant of success is organisational learning and a culture where people work together and are fully committed to the organisation's goals.

Nowadays, in competitive industries organisational learning is a prerequisite for organisational success. Many successful companies such as Google, Apple and Ebay are perfect examples and role models of effective organisational learning and culture. The notion organisational learning is a relatively new concept and it took very long that the people realise the importance of it. In the past employees were not seen as human beings, rather they were considered machines as a means to an end.

In the century that followed the upswing of the industrial age, management theorists such as Henri Fayol, F. W. Mooney or Lyndall Urwick were the first proponents of what we know as the classical management theory, which could be described as *a pattern of precisely defined jobs organized in a hierarchical manner through precisely defined lines of command and communication.* (Morgan, 2006, p. 18)

Nowadays, it might be argued that the management principles advocated by the great theorists of the last century were utterly wrong, because in most cases they made an organisation working like a machine and inhibited creativity and innovation. Indeed, the ever increasing globalisation and the improvement of new technologies such as the Internet seem to significantly influence the perception and behaviour of individuals and organisations respectively. These new circumstances require rethinking, as *difference today lies in the rapidity of change and the increasingly unpredictable nature of the environment* (Pearn et al, 1995, p. 35).

In fact, it is the learning organisation which has the necessary capabilities to effectively adapt to environment change, which was described by Peter Senge in his book "The Fifth Discipline". But what distinguishes a learning organisation from its competitors? Broadly, the learning organisation is the one which looks into the future and considers long-term strategies, rather than focusing on the present and the short-term. It tries to figure out the underlying causes of events to solve problems effectively and learn from mistakes, rather than just relieving symptoms. Moreover, and probably most important, a learning organisation emphasises and recognises that employees are its most valuable asset to ensure sustainable development and innovation (Senge, 2006). As Gary Hamel put it, *for the first time since the dawning of the industrial age, the only way to build a company thats fit for future is to build one thats fit for human beings.* (The Economist, 2009, p. 84)

In fact, there are various theories about individual and organisational learning. One of the important and widely accepted theories comes from Argyris and Schn. They highlight the importance of organisation learning since organisational errors should not be undiscovered and it ought to be eliminated before it adversely affects the whole organisation. Single loop learning is when *given or chosen goals, values, plans and rules are operationalized rather than questioned.* While double loop *occurs when error is detected and corrected in ways that involve the modification of an organizations underlying norms, policies and objectives.* (Smith, 2001) In fact, the double loop is much complex since it is crucial to analyse the internal operations and the environment where the company is placed in order to effectively avoid mistakes and how to improve establishments. It is vital to ask questions about the organisation's goal and missions, consider the strategic plans, rather asking if the company provide the appropriate product (Leading Creatives, 2010). As seen, double loop learning is going in much more depth than single loop learning. But to adopt the double loop learning approach is easier said than done. For instance, employees who are working for a particular organisation for ages might think that they are working for this company for a long time and nothing bad happens.

Senge believes that individuals have difficulties to grab a big picture, because most of them don't think beyond their own position. This deficiency is exemplified by the seven learning disabilities, which are:

1. I am my position
2. The enemy is out there
3. The illusion of taking charge
4. The fixation on events
5. The parable of the boiled frog
6. The delusion of learning from experience
7. The myth of the management team (Senge, 2006)

In order to prevent the learning disabilities it is vital to establish a culture where people are willing to work with each other and share knowledge and ideas. It is important that managers are open-minded and incorporate ideas of their employees. One of the most important aspects in terms of organisational learning is listening carefully what employees say instead of ignoring it.

Meg Withman, the former CEO of eBay, the world's biggest e-commerce company, made a remarkable contribution to eBay's success with regard to her exceptional leadership competences. She is well-known *for listening carefully to her employees and expects her managers to do the same* (Johnson, et al, 2008, p. 129). Withman always stressed the role of employees as the most important asset every company has and that it is essential to uncover the full potential of employees to run a successful business. In addition, a suitable work environment has a unique influence on employee behaviour and leads to greater motivation, flexibility and creativity. That's the reason why eBay offers a great number of employee benefits that make a major contribution to its friendly and trustworthy environment. The workforce receive a variety of insurances such as medical and dental, complimentary snacks and beverages, summer picnics, fitness centre and massage and the possibility to meet executive team members and many more (eBay Careers, 2010).

As seen, eBay is fully aware of the role of its employees but if you really want to make use of the full potential of your employees, the above mentioned benefits are not enough. Rather it is important to give everyone a chance to contribute ideas and

let them feel that these ideas are taken seriously. eBay's approach to getting employees excited and motivation about new possibilities is to foster innovation through an internal Demo Expo where employees get the opportunity to present new features and applications (Jenkins, 2007). eBay doubtless understood that *some of the most effective consultants your organization could ever hire are already working for you* (Clemmer et al, 1990, p. 69).

This procedure can help to uncover the full potential of employees and gain new insights and ideas. It encourages employees to learn together and this is vital, since *there has never been a greater need for mastering team in learning organizations than there is today* (Senge, 2006, p. 219). In addition, constructive feedback is given to the workforce about their ideas, which encourage discussion and sharpens thinking. An additional benefit of feedback sessions is to show appreciation of employees' individual efforts (Jenkins, 2007) which ensures a smooth flow of ideas within the organisation and limits the fear not being taken seriously.

eBay's Demo Expo clearly shows that *employees themselves more often than not, know what needs to be done to improve operation* (Moss Kanter, 1985, p. 64). Therefore it would be a mistake to ignore the potential of employees. However, many managers tend to forget that a human being is of great value and hence shouldn't be seen as a means to an end. Without doubt today's businesses require employee commitment and trust to ensure success and growth. As Senge reminds us, *collectively, we can be more insightful, more intelligent than we can possibly be individually.* (Senge, 2006, p. 221)

In fact, training and development does not have to be a formal seminar which has to be carried out by an external consultancy, instead, it takes place within the company where mutual learning occurs without the contribution of a third party.

For example, the successful internet company Google is considered the second most innovative and also the second most admired organisation in the world (BusinessWeek, 2010; Fortune, 2010). Yet this is not enough, Google was also awarded as the best employer in the UK in 2008 (Great Place to Work, 2008). Without question, in order to remain competitive Google needs to be creative and innovative all the time in order to outpace their rivals. But what is Google's formula of success? In fact, despite Google's size it attempts to maintain a small company

atmosphere. Yet when a company grows quickly, it's more difficult to allow people to be creative" (Lowe, 2009, p. 158). To overcome this Google's leaders prefer to hold regular meetings where employees have the opportunity to come up with new ideas. In order to foster the idea generation process they introduced the twenty percent rule, which Google adopted from 3M, a multinational conglomerate. The reason why 3M introduced this rule was to avoid high turnover rates among their engineers (Girard, 2009).

The 20/80 percent rule is where Google engineers *can use 20 percent of their time to pursue personal projects they're passionate about* (Google, 2010) and "eighty percent of their time is dedicated to assigned projects" (Girard, 2009, p. 64). Hence, the 20 percent rule allows Google's engineers to unleash their creativity and ideas. This is exemplified by various popular products like Gmail, Google News, Google maps and so forth, which were created by engineers. As a result, Google's employees contribute to new innovations and help it to grow further. Likewise, employees might be faithful to the organisation since the employer appreciates employees' commitment. Without question, it is crucial to listen to people carefully since they might have a breakthrough idea.

For example, Alexander Graham Bell who invented the first telephone in the year 1875, faced outright dismissal from the incumbent Western Union, which argued that the invention is of no commercial value even though it was a technological breakthrough. In effect, after twenty years there were five million telephones in the US. Furthermore, American Telephone and Telegraph prospered and eventually became the largest organisation in the US (Tidd and Bessant, 2009).

This example shows that it is of great importance to listen to people and think about their ideas more seriously, well before they are inclined to share their ideas with another company or start a business on their own. As Louis Pasteur reminds us, "chance favours the prepared mind" (Welter and Egmon, 2006, p. 1).

Another important aspect to foster innovation and creativity is team working. The most innovative and admired company in the world Apple Inc. (BusinessWeek, 2010; Fortune, 2010) places much emphasis on communication, open-mindedness and collaboration, where employees are encouraged to express their ideas. According to Steve Jobs *it's ad hoc meetings of six people called by someone who*

thinks he has figured out the coolest new thing ever and who wants to know what other people think of his idea (Burrows, 2004). Furthermore, it is essential that employees share the company's vision. Matt Kingdon, chairman of "?What If!", an innovation consultancy, stresses that a company's vision and purpose are the "lifeblood of innovation energy." If you expect employees to be fully committed to what a company does, to be willing to put in many hours and even work on weekends, you need to make sure that they "*like what the body corporate is going for* and feel proud being part of it."(Tidd and Bessant, 2009, p. 133) As Trott (2002, p. 78) reminds us: *Creative people will be attracted those companies that themselves are viewed as creative.*

As a matter of fact, Apple distinguishes between rank-and-file employees who are given clear-cut directives as well as close supervision, and its proven talents who get a freer hand. Apple gives its talented and creative employees freedom they need in order to create amazing products. Furthermore, two times a week the design and engineering group have regular meetings in order to come up with new ideas, discuss particular ideas in depth and how they might be realised (Walters, 2008). This is an example of a situated learning approach where *learning takes place within a social framework of participation whereby individuals construct their own meaning through collaboration and interaction with others* (Sadler-Smith, 2006, p. 124). In the end, the best ideas from Apple's team meetings are presented to the management team, whereas individuals are entitled to make a contribution in order to avoid future mistakes (Walters, 2008). Without question, engaging team members in the decision making process is essential, as this *actually builds teamwork and improves the likelihood of acceptance and implementation.* (Tidd and Bessant, 2009, p. 128)

As seen, Apple places value on their employees since they are encouraged to be creative, innovative and contribute to organisational success. A setback for Apple is that they do not offer any relevant training opportunities. Rather employees have to gain new knowledge on their own (Glassdoor, 2010). However, Apple is considered as one of the most innovative company around the globe and they easily manage their employees without any further training establishments. In fact, it is crucial to

establish a culture, where people are willing to expand their knowledge on their own and learn together."

As can be seen from the previous examples, training and development is admittedly significant, but when it comes to a recession, there are opportunities in order to save costs. But only if managers see the importance of organisational learning and establish a trustworthy work atmosphere then they can save capital. Of course, *Strong leadership is required, but then that is always a requirement, even when we're not in a recession*□(CIPD, 2009). Also a learning organisation has numerous advantages if organisations take it seriously. They can gain competitive advantage over their rivals and ensure success and prosperity from a long term perspective. As Arie de Geus, the former head of Shell, reminds us, □*the ability to learn faster than your competitors may be the only sustainable competitive advantage*□(Senge, 2006, p. 4)."

In conclusion, training and development becomes more and more significant since most organisations operate in a fast changing and competitive environment. In order to keep up with industry standards, employees need to expand their skills and knowledge which can be accomplished by various training activities. But this is not enough, since training is not the only one aspect in order to undergo the recession. Especially when an economic downturn occurs employees need support and vice versa the organisation cannot survive without their workforce. In fact, it is crucial that organisations involve their employees in the decision making processes because they might come up with excellent new ideas. Another significant aspect is that the employers understand the importance of mutual learning. All these leads to competitive advantage over rivals and can help that the organisation prospers. It goes without saying that organisational learning and culture should be embraced even if there is no recession. The companies Apple, eBay and Google lead by example because they establish an atmosphere where employees can share their ideas with the top management team, have the opportunity to dedicate on their own projects, receive further incentives and bonuses and many more. The three world-famous organisations also highlight the importance of effective team working which fosters creativity and innovation. As Mattie Stephanek put it, □*Unity is strength...*

when there is teamwork and collaboration, wonderful things can be achieved
(Livingston, 2008, p. 137).

References

Ambition (2010) *The importance of staff training during the recession. [Online]*
Available at: http://www.ambition.co.uk/news/featured-articles/the-importance-of-staff-training-during-the-recession.asp (Accessed: 19 November 2010)

Burrows P. (2004) "The Seed of Apple's Innovation", *BusinessWeek* [Online].
Available at:
http://www.businessweek.com/bwdaily/dnflash/oct2004/nf20041012_4018_PG2_db0
83.htm (Accessed: 21 November 2010)

Businessweek (2010) *The 25 Most Innovative Companies 2010. [Online]*
http://images.businessweek.com/ss/10/04/0415_most_innovative_companies/25.htm
(Accessed: 11 November2010)

Businessweek (2010) *The 25 Most Innovative Companies 2010. [Online]*
http://images.businessweek.com/ss/10/04/0415_most_innovative_companies/26.htm
(Accessed: 11 November 2010)

CIPD (2009) *Innovative Learning and Talent Development. [Online]*
Available at: http://www.cipd.co.uk/NR/rdonlyres/3C59B0CD-FC99-45A6-9D14-
88301ADCBF39/0/Innovative_learning_talent_development.pdf (Accessed: 21
November 2010)

Clarke, A. (2001) *Learning Organisations.*
Leicester: National Institute of Adult Continuing Education

Clemmer J. and Sheehy B. (1990) *Firing on all cylinders.*
London: Macmillan of Canada

Ebay Careers (2010) *Benefits.*
Available at: http://www.ebaycareers.com/benefits.html (Accessed: 9 November
2009)
(Accessed: 21 November 2010)

Glassdoor (2010) *Apple Reviews.*
Available at: http://www.glassdoor.com/Reviews/Apple-Reviews-E1138.htm
(Accessed: 21 November 2010)

Great Place to Work UK (2008) *2008 UKs 50 Best Workplace. [Online]*
http://www.greatplacetowork.com/best/list-uk-2008.htm (Accessed: 11 November
2010)

Fortune (2010) *Worlds most admired companies. [Online]*
Available at: http://money.cnn.com/magazines/fortune/mostadmired/2010/full_list/
(Accessed: 21 November 2010)

Girard, B. (2009) *The Google Way.*
San Francisco: No Starch Press, Inc.

Google (2010) *Google is looking for people with great aspirations. [Online]*
Available at: http://www.google.com/rec/dreamindia/ (Accessed: 21 November 2010)

Jenkin K. (2007) *eBays internal Demo Expo taps into employee creativity.[Online]*
Available at: http://karenjenkin.com/2007/06/05/ebays-internal-demo-expo-taps-into-
employee-creativity/ (Accessed: 21 November 2010)

Johnson G., Scholes K., Whittington R. (2008) *Exploring Corporate Strategy.*
8. edn Harlow: Pearson Education Ltd.

Leading Creatives (2010) *Double Loop Learning. [Online]*
Available at: http://www.leadingcreatives.com/2010/04/double-loop-learning.html
(Accessed: 21 November 2010)

Livingston, B. (2008) *How you do... What you do.*
New York: McGrawHill

Lowe, J. (2009) *Google speaks: Secrets of the World's Greatest Billionaire Entrepreneurs, Sergey Brin and Larry Page.* New Jersey: John Wiley & Sons, Inc.

Martin, M. and Jackson, T. (2002) *Personnel Practice.* 3rd edn. London: Chartered Institute of Personnel and Development

Morgan G. (2008) *Images of Organization.* London: SAGE Publications Ltd.

Moss Kanter, R. (1985) *The Change Masters.* London: Unwin Hyman Ltd.

Pearn M., Roderick C. and Mulrooney C. (1995) *Learning Organizations in practice.* Maidenhead: McGraw-Hill Book Company Europe

Sadler-Smith, E. (2006) *Learning and Development for Managers.* Oxford: Blackwell Publishing

Senge, P. (2006) *The fifth discipline.* London: Random House

Smith, M.K. (2001) "Peter Senge and the learning organization", *Infed. [Online]* Available at: http://www.infed.org/thinkers/senge.htm (Accessed: 29 October 2010)

Smith, M.K. (2001) "Chris Argyris: Theories of Action, Double-Loop learning and Organisational Learning", *Infed. [Online]* Available at: http://www.infed.org/thinkers/argyris.htm (Accessed: 21 November 2010)

Strack, R., Caye, J.M., Thurner, R. and Haen, P. (2009) "Creating People Advantage in Times of Crisis", *Boston Consulting Group. [Online]* Available at: http://www.bcg.com/documents/file15224.pdf (Accessed: 21 November 2010)

The Economist (2009) *The three habits ...* 24th October 2009 Peterborough: St Ives plc

The Economist (2007) *Inside the Googleplex. [Online]* http://www.economist.com/displaystory.cfm?story_id=9719610&source=login_payBa rrier (Accessed: 21 November 2010)

Tidd, J. and Bessant, J. (2009) *Managing Innovation.* 4th edn. West Sussex: John Wiley & Sons Ltd.

Walters H. (2009) "Jonathan Ive on the Key to Apple's Success", *BusinessWeek* [Online]. Available at: http://www.businessweek.com/innovate/next/archives/2009/07/jonathan_ive_th.html (Accessed: 21 November 2010)

Welter, B. and Egmon, J. (2006) *The prepared mind of a leader.* San Francisco: Jossey-Bass